Portrait in a Spoon

Publication of this book was supported by a grant from the Eric Mathieu King Fund of The Academy of American Poets.

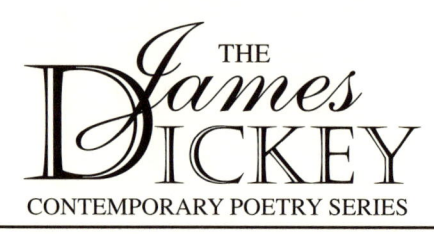

THE James
DICKEY
CONTEMPORARY POETRY SERIES

EDITED BY RICHARD HOWARD

Portrait in a Spoon

Poems by
James Cummins

UNIVERSITY OF SOUTH CAROLINA PRESS

© 1997 James Cummins

Published in Columbia, South Carolina, by the
University of South Carolina Press

Manufactured in the United States of America

01 00 99 98 97   5 4 3 2 1

Library of Congress Cataloging-in-Publication Data

Cummins, James.
   Portrait in a spoon : poems / by James Cummins.
      p.   cm. — (The James Dickey contemporary poetry series)
   ISBN 1–57003–191–6 (CL). — ISBN 1–57003–192–4 (PB)
   I. Title. II. Series.
PS3553.U455P6 1997
811'.54—dc21   97–4723

For Katherine,
my light

Contents

III. Foolish Countenances

A Note on James Cummins

As a literary phenomenon, as a category of received po-
etical circumstance, the Second Book—particularly when
a poet's First has been notable and nonesuch—calls for spe-
cial regard: poems here are likely to be found closer to the
bone (what is criticism, after all, but in the wisdom of our
etymology a cutting-at-the-joints?) than those incipient per-
formances wherein the flagrant distractions of merely mak-
ing inveterately loomed or lowered somewhat *apart*. It is
these ensuing texts—anything but *secondary* except in the
temporal dimension—which tend to incarnate what the poet
can do rather than what is but obligatory, but needful to get
poems written *in the first place*.

As first books come and go, James Cummins made some-
thing of a sensation, a few years back, with *The Whole Truth,*
which many readers gleefully characterize as "the Perry
Mason sestinas"; a relentless, sometimes goofy, and always
graphic sequence wherein the dread concepts of plot and
character were goaded through the most unyielding formal
baffles that occidental poetry has yet devised. Virtuosity
emerged, even protruded, as the justification which mod-
esty proposes in such cases, an expedient of *desperate mea-
sures.*

In the present instance, an alleviated reader will find,
still, a few inevitably expert sestinas, as well as poems ("Por-
tals" is a good example) that appear to be convalescing from
sestination; but for the most part—and for the best part, it
seems to me—these subsequent Cummins poems require
far less tending, many fewer props and struts in order to
articulate their identity, their essential pain (their essential
pleasure: all one, as the poet reminds us). It is, that iden-
tity, the matter and the (sometimes grand) manner of a rel-
ished solitude, for all the jokes at the expense of Rival Poets,

Star Athletes, and Family Counsellors, and for all the voiced (or under-voiced) claims that it is dark in here, and cold, and wet, and hard to breathe . . . *Sotto voce* stage directions from the heart, the lungs, and what used to be called the liver and lights.

Henry James remarked somewhere in *The American Scene* that New England villages afforded so little possibility of "conversation" that introspection had become a social resource; Cummins makes us realize that in southern Ohio, loneliness is a spectator sport, a recreation in which he may triumph over Rilke and Hemingway, Hamlet and Jackson Pollock, to name but the big-league contenders. Family and Profession are the easy losers here, and not even a new daughter can offer much in the way of competition:

> . . . you'll know what I know,
> the sadness of most things a little before
> their beauty.

Of course it is love, famous opponent of all our solitudes, that Cummins has *really* seen through, the inevitable result of such transparency being that no matter how many may give themselves to this lover, no matter how many he may take, there is always a third party to their intercourses—the third party is time, which makes cuckolds of them both:

> We sit in middle age, the snapped-
> off languages lying close,
> like toys we have succeeded
> in demolishing. Will touch
> proceed from this, or scorn—
>
> scorn of the human? And that's
> the story within the story:
> the scorn or love that once
> were different, yet now
> mean one and the same thing.

Cummins's odd and entirely appropriate title for his new book frames the enterprise between the inevitable solitary reflections; he begins with George Eliot's derision of "various small mirrors," extending to "Milton, looking for his portrait in a spoon," an inevitable source of grotesque likeness, and he ends with the classical adjuration to his book:

> Go, little mirror. You hold up to me
> only desire, not what I long to see.

Of course by laying (pressing?) so much weight on the heartbreak of the matter, I have badly neglected the hilarity; Cummins is a genuinely funny poet, though not a comical one—it always hurts when he laughs—it hurts *us*.

Richard Howard

Acknowledgments

Grateful acknowledgment is made to the editors of the following magazines, in which some of these poems first appeared:

Antioch Review
"The Brother"

Chariton Review
"Guides"
"Romantic Love"

Kenyon Review
"Reading Hemingway"
"White Rose"

Paris Review
"An *Ars Poetica* for You"
"'Schindler's List'"
"Fling" (original title "Sestina")
"The Body Is the Flower" (original title "Sestina")
"To My Daughter"
"The Voices"

Ploughshares
"The Poet-in-Residence"

Poetry Northwest
"Gambler's Death"

Shenandoah
"A Biography"
"The Imaginary Friendship of Li Ho and Tu Mu"

Western Humanities Review
"Good-bye to All That"
"Outside the Paul Laurence Dunbar House, the Grifter
   Sees Us Coming"
"Turista"

"The Body Is the Flower" appeared in *Best American
Poetry 1994,* under its original title, "Sestina."

"Fling" appeared in *Best American Poetry 1995,* under its
original title, "Sestina."

I would like to thank the National Endowment for the Arts
and the Ingram Merrill Foundation for literary fellowships
and the University of Cincinnati for a sabbatical leave, all
of which supported the making of parts of this book.

I am not sure that the greatest man of his age . . . could escape these unfavorable reflections of himself in various small mirrors; and even Milton, looking for his portrait in a spoon, must submit to have the facial angle of a bumpkin.

George Eliot, *Middlemarch*

I

A Biography

Gambler's Death

It was only a matter of time and windows,
give or take an ashtray.
He revolved like a duck in a gallery,
but slowly, past the windows:
business office, teller, race track . . .
in the year of the proposal of money.

He woke each morning to his face
stamped on a coin he'd put up above
the sink to help him shave:
when it moved, his blade clicked off
the whiskers like turnstiles—
the absence of money was like age.

He discovered a woman sleeping within him
like the thought of himself
on a certain day of his youth.
He drifted, a boat unmoored,
in the realm of her gaze as he watched
his hand float toward his soft drink at lunch,

or rest on the wheel at a stoplight.
At night, in the driveway, the car door open
for light, his eyes sometimes lifted
from the racing form spread open,
its numbers and times like the muted
knowing talk of trainers, jockeys,

of owners who drove beneath the green trees
in blacks cars each Saturday morning,
handing out money like elegant,
unapproachable gestures of duty, success,
the quiet assurance of age—
and he would think, for seconds, he saw her,

someone he had never seen, but felt,
as he suddenly felt the darkness carry
the last shouts of a children's game
into him, more remembered than heard,
filling the car with a terrible longing
for the family he saw behind the lit windows.

Each night it seemed it took longer
to get there, that living room.
Then a dream of a white, forgotten end—
the bed folding its rectangular ghost
about him like a bad hand, keeping
the scream from his throat, his eyes

mirroring his son's face like lemons—
glimmering, sinking, and no jackpot:
his gaze around the room, each doorway
releasing one of his family, each window
a welcoming handshake and bluff greeting—
and he too old for the shows of such strength.

The Voices

Because I evinced an interest a few
of the younger doctors bought me a white
coat. It was quite a joke (there was even
some discussion of rubber instruments),
and I went along with it, often jamming
my hands into my pockets and dancing
around the room, humming "The Blue Danube."
I enjoyed them: they were so much funnier
than the older ones with their monocles.
Usually, we stood around imitating
the more severely afflicted patients,
or just cracking jokes: "Take Napoleon.
Please." I had a room with a river view—
it's surprising what an honest appraisal
of one's needs can avail—and my photos
of celebrities caught in compromising
positions (which I'd blown up to poster size)
became rather the rage. I acquired
a sort of cult following. They gave me
a nameplate and began to smuggle me
into the Staff Cafeteria—until
within a few years, the turnover rate
nearly as high as the one for suicide,
no one remained among the attendants
who remembered I'd once been a patient.
Eventually, I was given an office

and then formally welcomed to the staff.
No one was more surprised than I (which
distraction, along with the forged photostats
of my doctorate from Chicago, was taken
as the air of genius). I grew accustomed
to this respectful attitude. I became
quite a team player: I found I had a knack
for keeping everyone "loose." Thus it was
I came to know my true calling: I
could see behind the fused mask of healing.
There were rooms leading into rooms. In each,
a child played with her toys, or dressed in his
mother's clothes, or squinted along the barrel
of a toy rifle, dreaming of getting
a father in its sights . . . Amazing: it was
all true, what they said—yet they were
left in the ruins of their discoveries,
and no good came of them. At the staff dinners,
which I more and more often prepared,
the jokes about "a mother's touch" became—
more accurately so—blurts of pain and fear,
unsurrounded by laughter. More than once,
after too much wine, I held someone's head
to my breasts, stroking the damp hair . . .
But soon after I purchased the ham radio,
we all became buffs. So many stories,
out there, to be listened to—and perhaps
downstairs, in one's own living room, someone
sits, and will not listen. We listened.
And made suggestions. Although we had only

speech patterns, and a safe anonymity
to go on, the painful lesions and trauma
are evident to the intuitive mind.
There was "Eskimo"—a man who lived in
Juneau, and was a high school teacher.
(He called his Buick a dogsled, to amuse us.)
"Thick Wrists" was an ex-auto racer.
And "Buckeye" was a housewife in Ohio
who had lived for some years in Indiana
and was afraid she would become known as
a "Hoosier." (That was an interesting case.)
But there were many cases: radio signals
coming in from all over the country.
And it was through listening to them
I grew to be very happy in my work.
In the mornings, I see my patients—
for though I but dimly remember my own
illness, I am unable to deny them.
No, more: I need them. In the afternoons,
I read and write in my rooms overlooking the river.
And in the evening we gather
in the large room at the end of the hall
to listen to the voices we take care of.
I am happy. Yet often at night when
I'm certain the others are asleep,
I close the door to my room softly,
get some milk in the kitchen—it calms me—
and sit down in front of the radio,
working its dials. I speak to the numberless
voices I don't know, and give and receive

small bits of useful information.
Someone has a recipe, or has seen
a good movie—perhaps an amusing
story about a child. I know now I'm not
looking for anyone, anymore. No one
is left, whose voice I don't understand.
For my own mother is dead, and though I
don't know where she has gone, I know where
she has been—and I hear the stories
surrounding me as they once surrounded her.
They rise up so beautifully some nights,
opening like a bright fan of pain—
and what is left of her voice is a darkness
turning in my mind like a diamond
turning in the kidney of a bum, his cry . . .
I hear it, and close my eyes, and can sleep.

A Biography

Don't tell me of that city:
I could have died there.

I thought of my body as its river—
drifting, colorless, thrown wrong

along, into, that historic earth—
and of the river as shoulders

drenched in perfume like the scent
of a woman my father once had,

who beckoned to me with my own arms,
the arms I had lent her, to hold him.

I thought of myself as that river,
the look I had as the seasons changed:

the trees were my changing moods;
the drift of a cloud, a desire—

each slowing in the gesture of a year . . .
My face in the water was no face,

a face in storefronts I walked by,
in order to study its thin argument,

a face I engraved on tears I sold,
only to be selling tears: the moon

was my face, as I lay on my back
in my bed, between two cities—

I could look down on myself,
the pitiable wreckage of boats

I had learned, from her, to lure
with a song borrowed from her throat,

the neck I was a pain in when,
at night, for a joke, we would die . . .

Then, I would get up, my arms thin, milky,
transparent in the moonlight, my body

her own shadow struggling against itself:
me . . . This is how I learned to walk,

how I learned to glide, soft as water,
down those black ropes to their ends,

the stories I listened to there,
at the end of a city street.

The Imaginary Friendship
of Li Ho and Tu Mu

1. *Li Ho Speaks*

What's in a name, you ask, unhappily.
Or a face? I reply, and giggle.

The form did not encase me like a hard birth,
but was like a fetus in me I was moved to expel.

I was sure there was a door, early in the corridor,
decorated with the most beautiful designs of jade,
that opened to a room with couches of burnished gold,
upon whose cushions I might have relaxed, been brought
    food—

for I have read of this, and have been moved to tears.
But I went on looking for someone, I know not whom,
though I knew it was not you for whom I searched.

2. *Tu Mu Replies*

I only knew to offer myself.
Had I been a General I would have sacrificed many men
in a vain attempt to capture the besieged town.
But I am a civil servant: the stylized gesture, the eyes
furious to have been left behind by the body.

Certainly there are colors
beyond the dialectic

of frenzy and boredom. I listen
to the janitors, all about forty,
make jokes about the clerks, in their formal dress.

I believed the light
entering my body at different points
formed, inside, a mirror
in which a child slept,
and before which a grown man wondered.

As if pain were not the experience,
but the seeking after . . .

The Beloved

At dinner, his face a bag of food,
his wife speaks:
"Look at his polished palms
held upward, at his sides,

as if expecting rain. He hasn't
worked a day in his life,
and people make him pay for it."
He eats a special cracker

that she buys for him
in the special crackers section,
then wraps his mouth around
a container of milk. "Marvin's just

like me," he says of a successful friend.
"The only time he sweats
is upon the occasion of ridicule,
or the possibility of sex."

And he is willing to throw
his face down into a plate of food.
His wife has taught him to cry and wave
his arms as if drowning,

then admit more wrong than anyone:
"Wisdom is just a tooth the wise
man loses. Whose fear oozes
from his pores as mine does?"

Gift

Lack of sleep thins you
to a blue stick,
as a painted slide box
hides a nickel.

Someone lives alone.
She is old enough
to know better, too
young to resist.

You think of her,
naked, showered,
begin to know something
of your own skin.

She brings you a gift.
Your hands plunge
through tissue paper
to get at it . . .

A thin membrane
between this nakedness
and that desire,
what can be given you?

As a lacquered box
fitting in one hand
slides its circle forward,
and in it, her face.

Nights

It wasn't a seduction. Or perhaps that was what seduction meant: the winding passage one takes to reach love. About them whorled the winds of protest, consciousness; but here, in the cove of this room, they protested in their own silent ways against the private tyrannies that kept them from a knowledge of themselves, and of each other.

Even in their delicate movements about each other, their positions stemmed from basic roles: pursuer, pursued. He'd believed once that this could be talked about. Here she was, taking this condescending attitude without even knowing it, hoping he would know something she didn't: how to get to her. Were they attracted to each other because each accepted as a ground rule something having to do with perfection? If the journey were successful, a gold cup would pour forth an infinite amount of liquid, a deep spring would gush forth life-giving water endlessly. If it were not successful . . . it would be a small bottle, of liquor, perhaps hidden in a medicine cabinet, to which they would return a number of times until, drained, dry, it no longer nourished them; or worse, became a symbol itself, throwing into a clear light by its perversity that very perfection which had not been, and could not now be, attained.

He felt if he got up and went to the window to watch the lights of the street, the darkness would swirl between them like an ocean, sweeping them apart as they called frantically to each other, until they disappeared or drowned. He wouldn't risk it, having foreseen it, yet something did impel him toward the window. A vague anger, frustration, as if it were always up to him to speak, to offer, to throw the line in

more ways than one. He rebelled against her, and his rebel-
lion pulled him away. Darkness flowed between them in an
inch-wide river, then a foot.

He lay there, sweating, thinking of C., who had screamed
at him, and of D., at whom he had screamed.

Marriage Songs

1

The figure entering
shrank almost instantly;
or the cavern expanded—
it was hard to tell.

The shadow thrown along
the pitch wall
by a small candle
groped with shadow hands
along the wet surface;

or suddenly it would be
too tight for the tiny
body to breathe,
grown horribly large.

There was no mirror
but the thought of itself.
Its head lolled
like a walnut
on the panicked, constricted

mass; or swelled
to contain the scene
in which an inadequate arm

drew pictures in blood
on the dark wall.

Memory was its instrument
for measurement.
A broad sky,
its blue cape of stars,
arced over its passage.

That was the beginning
of the sentimental,
or the forgotten.
The body heaved, became

its tubular death; replaced
the shadow it grew into,
and lay down—
breathing, watching.

2

What he is allowed to speak of;
outlasting the night, and then
the light may not be turned on.

To husband is to witness;
husband and wife
carom in a game
of night-colored billiards;
what reticence
between her legs
does he perceive—

but she,
new testament to wildness
he is not up to?

A screaming left off . . .
Nothing was come to.
It was possible to hold
all in the mind
for a minute, an hour—
and to speak of it.
A way of going, perhaps, ahead . . .

Bodies hurtling, and hurting;
pine, maple, corn—
the earth gave off a clean smell
permeating the dusk, its
purple liqueur . . .

Underside of peppermint,
wintergreen.
Large areas of soil
under which no bodies have lain.

3

Wanting his death
has not come to her
yet.
        Stem, bending
beneath the weight
of the flower:

what is it held
them down, what
do they stretch up
into?

There is
a way to begin
for anyone; you
must find it.
It appears first

as constriction,
womb, cave
in which no breath
is possible.

It is
sheath, walls
of chlorophyll
stretching

into the future.

Entrails

These insults, leaves, kisses,
ovens opening with food for thought,
an unlaced boot that remains
in a room from which the furniture
was taken years ago, the same
tree knocking against the window,
pushed by a green, windy light.

One stands up into something.
Perhaps as a king threading his arms
through a jacket held by a servant;
perhaps as an innocent condemned man,
who wants only to strike, and quickly.

She lay on the couch, head twisted
back over a shoulder, eyes open
enough that a black bead fell out.
This was all the accusation she
could muster, hand between her legs.

Mirrors had lost their usefulness.
It became a mirror to hold one up,
pretending to shock at its contents.
They rubbed against each other
in separate flames, never becoming,
after all, the one flame that leads
the body through the dark of sex.

The horse was found strangled,
smothered in his feed bag, every oat
in his mouth, even the ones he had
been unable, at the last, to chew.
It was considered a sign.

Hamlet Relieves Himself

Let the face relax, behind its iron. Stand tall.
Dear Polonius still gives me his good advice.
I love those old ones, lucky enough to die.
To be stabbed in the back by a friend is treachery,
but to die from it bespeaks a goodness all its own.
Not that I'd let them get me from behind.
Only an old fool trusts his friends.

Hamlet at Work

In the morning that I can bounce
out beaming from the shower,
tying a tie, perhaps,
making my way through bus,
office, day, among
the co-conspirators, loves—

do they not hear
the crass scream inside me,
do they fail to notice
what I can become
after, say, a cup
or two of coffee,
and a sugar bun?

Rape, pillage, destruction—
among the many, I brush
my teeth, keep my nose
clean, and moan at night,
thinking of them.

Hamlet Drinks with His Buddy, Tom

"How many of you dance on the head of a pin?"
I asked her this in all sincerity. How would I know
mullings of one era are wisecracks in another?
She tossed her hair. "Or sit on a pinhead's face?"
The lusty wench . . . I understood the fire in her eyes
better than her words: "Not a ghost of a chance!"
But how to approach her? What scarf could I carry
as the silk of my intentions? I'm not a doubting man,
Aquinas, though a name thrills through my blood, too,
with its signals from the past. (As well you knew,
searching a more abstract palm for its tell-tale hole.)
We wander, Thomas, if we go or stay, but we dance
if we but lift our eyes. We danced, seeing the future.
And by God, Tom, you old croak, I knew. Two.

Overheard

"And what if I cried, perhaps not
among the angels, but here, right
here, in your kitchen?

Would it be a break, a rupture?
Frightening in its extent, its
threat? The domino theory:

would we begin to fall like small
Asian countries, against the
stove, pushing a table chair

toward the back door as we sank,
hands along our temples,
swooning, awestruck before the

light? At twenty, we liked
writhing around on the floor
with each other, but at forty

we cut each other off and up,
we know another body is no
door against the cold wind,

we don't open. So would I take
what you might offer instead?
Or would I turn away, ashamed

you saw my mouth slack, self-
absorbed, my eyes begging for
it, some kindness it tortured your

soul to extend? What bargain
can we strike now, love, and what
angel would witness the deal?"

To My Daughter

Who knows what we will ask of you, need of you?
Who would know why, if I sat up next to your bed
for hours each night, robbing you of the dark,
and you too tired, of course, but registering
each little crescent of light behind each eyelid?
And perhaps it will be in that mild irritation
we will make our first connection, maybe you
will grow to resent this intrusion on your sleep,
and you will wait patiently your entire life
to find that word, whatever words will make
me miserable for a year, but you more free
to breathe and walk in the sun your short while.
You will come out of me, you know, then.
The years of hovering around you, I hope
benignly, afraid that you will learn my fear,
make my mistakes, or that you'll know what I know,
the sadness of most things a little before
their beauty—these years like my arms will open,
and you will walk out no less tentative than
the morning you will stand up for the first time,
and move in a businesslike way from couch to table.
The old snake will accept the illusion of the skin,
turn into the paper of yesterday's papers for you,
that you might break clear: you'll see me again,
in another guise, before I leave you forever,
before you founder one night in a dark room,

not unlike this one, your thoughts far from me that drive you to your loneliness among others. Perhaps then some one time I tried to signal you will open before your eyes like the flower those moments were intended to be, and you will take some comfort again in knowing that I loved you. Who knows what we will ask of you, need of you?

II

The Men's Room

Fling

He wanted to tell her the weekend idea was "neat,"
But he kept hearing himself repeat the word "funny."
She named the names of trees, flowers: *sycamore, tulip.*
He asked her who did she think she was, Gary Snyder?
Above the car, then over the hotel, the spring moon
Was full, orange. "This isn't just another fling,"

She said suddenly. "Don't dare think it's some fling."
The Jack Daniel's arrived, hers on the rocks, his neat.
"I didn't think that at all." Behind her, the moon
Looked away. She fretted. "I just—I feel funny."
Amazingly, it occurred to him something Gary Snyder
Once said was appropriate. He repeated it. "Tulips,"

She smiled back. "Let's take a walk through the tulips."
Later, they didn't make love. She was shy. Some fling,
He brooded. Did she really think he *liked* Gary Snyder—
That he, too, thought he had it all summed up in a neat
Little package? Funny, he groaned. Worse than funny.
I get it all right, for once: drinks, room, even the moon

Cooperates. How often can you count on a spring moon
Slipping through the sycamores, picking out the tulips
In the night air? She should feel romantic, not "funny!"
Lying next to her, he felt so restless, eager to fling
His body atop hers—seeking, yet in control, his need
Ascetic, sensual, yet poised—a suburban Gary Snyder . . .

In the dark, she teased: "Thinking about Gary Snyder?"
Then: "I'm not so shy now." He thought about the moon,
And a Grace Paley character who "liked his pussy neat."
Then she was touching him, needing him, her two lips
Soft flowers, emissaries of her body, gently ruffling
Against him, moving him, so powerfully it wasn't funny . . .

Afterward, they were awkward, shy, trying to be funny.
They couldn't get any more mileage out of Gary Snyder.
"Some fling," he said, and she flung back, "Some fling!"
But mostly they were quiet. Outside, the big yellow moon
Yawned. He made a mental note to send her some tulips.
She stared out the window, thinking about the word "neat."

* * *

He thought of how she'd fling her hair. And the moon . . .
It was *finito*. Next week he got a book by Gary Snyder
In the mail. That was funny. He sent her the tulips.

Reading Hemingway

Reading Hemingway makes me so hungry,
for *jambon,* cheeses, and a dry white wine.
Cold, of course, very cold. And very dry.

Reading Hemingway makes some folks angry:
the hip drinking, the bitter pantomime.
But reading Hemingway makes me hungry

for the good life, the sun, the fish, the sky:
blue air, *white water,* dinner on the line . . .
Had it down cold, he did. And dry. Real dry.

But Papa had it all, the *brio,* the *Brie:*
clear-eyed, tight-lipped, advancing on a *stein* . . .
Reading Hemingway makes me so hungry,

I'd knock down Monsieur Stevens, too, if I
drank too much *retsina* before we dined.
(Too old, that man, and way too cold. And dry

enough to rub one's famished nerves awry,
kept talking past the kitchen's closing time!)
Reading Hemingway makes me so hungry . . .
And cold, of course. So cold. And very dry.

The Man Who Broke
Jackson Pollock's Nose

was a middle-aged man, not too terribly overweight,
though he obviously was fighting the battle of the bulge,
and as he sat drinking a beer with some friends in a booth,
he was both in and out of this world, and his own.

So when Jackson Pollock, over some God-knows-what
imagined slight, pushed his loud and belligerent bulk
right into the space and the face of this bitter,
recessive man, something snapped. Instantly,

he saw in this fearful, compulsive genius just what
this fearful, compulsive genius was looking for each night,
breaking and battering his way through his fame:
himself, his double, his *doppelgänger*, The Other Who Is Not.

And it was too much. To be Jackson Pollock's *doppelgänger*—
to realize that the Other you too have been searching for
with such fear, is not the Other at all, but the Original—
and you the struck-dumb copy, the resembler—the catcher,

for God's sake—well, it was too much. Something snapped,
and a right forearm shot out, unprepossessing but fired
by resentment no bulging bag of bullying whine,
no bounder with some feces-in-his-underwear desperation,

could begin to understand the rhyme or the reason of.
The hateful glare, teeth clenched, lurched toward him—
then it was reeling backward, a hand clutching at it,
and then it was gone, disappearing into the chaos and shouting.

So who confronted whom that night? For a few moments,
the nondescript hero sat with a silly smile on his face,
embarrassed, as if he were some sort of athletic champion,
the whispering around him filled with awe and admiration.

He'd been the one to stand up to the leering, the insinuation,
the self-inflection that inflicts itself on the meek,
on the weak, on the face that takes the fist as the bowl
of oatmeal takes the spoon. He'd been the one to draw

the line, speak the No, direct the force of the forceful
back against its hurt self. He lifted his rubbery arms
toward his beer, as the whispering grew louder, angrier,
and he realized nothing had changed, he had changed nothing,

he was merely an "incident" in the great artist's life,
not the reverse, never the reverse. The adrenaline left him
as quickly as it had come, and he slipped out into the night,
before the burly men who hoisted Pollock to the ambulance

returned, their outraged faces strobing back into the bar.
That he'd forgotten to pay his tab gave him some satisfaction,
but the memory of the punch—the thrusting, rigid
    potency of it—
well, they couldn't take that away from him, the memory.

Good-bye to All That

Let's tiptoe away from the lives of the men.
More and more, they are thinking less and less
of us, so let's think less and less of them.

We have to save ourselves; we can't save them.
Their football games, their need to be the "best":
let's tiptoe away from the lives of the men.

What makes them so afraid, when day is done?
What do they need to comprehend, confess?
Do they know we think less and less of them?

Look at the sneer on the embittered son;
or the father, pounding his hairy chest—
let's tiptoe away from the lives of the men.

They turn away from those they should attend,
then turn back to them, needing to be blessed.
Let's tiptoe away from the lives of the men;
already, we think less and less of them.

Quotes

". . . Nowadays, my dearest Greta, when boys
play war, it is still the call to adventure, still the
land of the hero, to be transmuted and trans-
formed in the crucible of experience. And with
comrades. How much easier is a headlong dash
to death, when you are young, and have com-
rades!"

> —Lieutenant Elijah Cook, Jr.,
> 1st Virginia Cavalry, CSA, 1861

"The Confederates were the last plumed Ameri-
cans. The Union boys who climbed
Fredericksburg hill wore no plumes."

> —Major John Ramsey Clark,
> retired, U.S. Army, 1895

"I see two men on horseback meet on a ridge.
What is the one key that unlocks the two
hearts? Perhaps a moment of acceptance, a
look that passes between them, that communi-
cates not only the understanding of a fellow
traveler, but also the sense that the endless
wheels and machinations of the universe fit
together in such a way as to make this moment
in time possible, that nothing is denied and all
is accepted in the presence of each other, just
as surely as each of them must return to his

own net of contingencies shortly. I imagine this is more rare than not, yet also not so rare as one might think, who wonders about his own ability humbly to accept and participate in such a moment."

—Colonel Morgan Hunt Freeman,
4th Texas Cavalry, CSA, 1865

"The trouble with Hooker is that he's got his headquarters where his hindquarters ought to be."

—President Abraham Lincoln, 1862

"Mother, when I said in my last letter that I wanted to describe the buildings, the way they stand so still and desolate after a battle, I was trying to describe a problem I have. It is the problem of a church standing in a quiet autumn field, without sound, no birds, no insects in the grass, the brilliant sun on the gold-red leaves. It is the problem of a schoolyard on a grey deserted Sunday afternoon, a bitter December wind coming in off the lake. The problem is that all man-made things carry with them an unspoken vanity and a corresponding despair. Dear Mother, how I long to be with you this night!"

—Letter found on the body of an unidentified Union soldier, Antietam, 1862

The Son

I want to break down,
back off from the voices
falling down like a father
coming home late, a mother
reading "anecdotes" aloud
from the *Reader's Digest*.
I ask my eyes to crack open,
like stones in a fire,
then, blinded, to return
to the burned-out warehouse,
the field behind the church,
smells of the dog hospital,
tar. I look at them,
frowning in the heat:
father, mother, first son
in his First Communion suit.
They agree to do what
they are told: he drives
his car, and does it well;
she rolls a white stocking
up her leg. He puts on
his yellow shoes, expecting
a crack from his boss;
she pushes the long pin
through her nurse's cap,
expecting nothing. They
agree to return, blinded,

to each other each night,
in all weather, for all reasons,
for none, as they were told.
I watch the summer thicken
in the squares of the screen.
I go outside, as I am told,
pick up a rusted can, or a ball,
begin to throw up my arms.

The Brother

The night I kissed you on the lips,
you lay back in my arms like a woman,
someone you had seen in a movie,
passive and appealing to a lover.
You were seven, and I was going
out of your life for a long time,
maybe forever. Your small body
suspected as much, and you lay back,
drawing my head down to your lips.
I see you yet, your thin legs
suddenly useless, sticking out
from my arms like a marionette,
a crash victim, a truncated me
made manifest in my arms as I
made plans to leave that house,
no good-byes to anyone, not even you.
I was eighteen, had carried you
up to bed each night for five years,
lifting you sleeping from the couch.
I held you as a father holds his son,
holds all he doesn't know he knows.
That night I saw it was this love
you longed for, that in your need
you would be anything, even a woman,
to soften my heart, to please me.
We will never reconcile. We spent
lavishly the love we had, lovers
who give no thought to the future.

The Husband

What can I say, and how can I say it?
That after years I no longer punish you,
yet neither do I wait for you, or hope?
That I sit at the dinner table with you,
and feel an honest affection as I watch you
read a newspaper, or a book, or talk?
We made a bargain not to leave each other,
struck at a level too deep even to mention
in argument, and we rarely argue anymore.
I want to keep you in sight, in view,
as boats call to each other across the water,
as geese mate for life in their high place,
as salmon will pursue their own undoing,
fallen into the cylinder of living, dying.
I have fallen into you, seen what I offered
as part of the pattern of your undoing—
I was too late to touch the flame, the flower,
that hung there, in that air. Does every
husband feel he is his wife's worst fate?
Is every married song one of apology?
I sit here, late at night, in my chair;
I am only a small cry of love to you.

The Poet

Like the flakings that become
short stories, novels,
letters to the editor,

the layers of fuck
yous, marital
positionings, personal

purgatories of friends
form, inside the poet,
uncommented on,

what forms in the oyster,
stroking and stroking
its inner self.

White Rose

Her hair is white now, like the mystic rose
she writes about without affect or ploy.
She burns, a meditation upon joy,
a joy whose darkness is the Self it chose.
Not Catherine of Siena's skull she sees,
nor some saint's finger bone in a gold case—
but what the skull and bone are to a face
and hand is what brings this rose to her knees.
"But ours is a profession," they complain.
"What good is bitterness"—her voice like birds—
"if God Himself denies a woman words?"
A joke, of course, yet in her eyes the pain.
For years they held promotions out of reach,
because she couldn't publish, only teach.

The Poet-in-Residence

He makes a myth of everything he does:
at dawn, he puts his shirt on—that's a poem.
At night, he takes it off—same deal. Alone,
he drinks to blot out the young man he was.
Oh, he was fine—muscles rippling, the fire
of subject matter in his eyes: his *home*
was what he wrote about, and sold, and none
outstared the staring of his righteous ire.
But now he stumbles in his drunken blues,
mocking himself, the word, the microphone—
ranting, prating his charming, tough-guy drone,
reduced to making art in interviews.
He spreads his thumb and forefinger, puckers:
"Suck this much cock, you're still a cocksucker."

Portrait of Man with Blue Mug

Tit, dick, toe: who knows what that mouth wants?
And wants, and wants? "It seems so bleak out there,"
it says, and she replies, "But we're in here.
What game is this? *Endgame?* Starring the Lunts?"
Bresson's priest, dying, whispers, "All is grace"—
denying himself, he finds himself at last.
Denying himself, our hero's time just passed:
self-effacement only led to loss of face.
Women auditioned for a part. Some knew.
But couldn't swell the progress of the play:
he didn't have the guts to go or stay;
he only had the gall to see it through.
To say that you were never loved requires
a mind that sees all women, men, as liars.

Games

A good athlete moves slowly after defeat,
or sits in the dugout staring at the field,
as it gets taken back by the ones who tend it,
who have nothing on their minds but the field,
they love it so. Some lights will blink out,
before he can enter the locker room again,
each face there reminding him of his loss,
his weakness, their weakness, at last exposed
when the final tally only mocked their ardor.
He is like a neophyte lover, exposed, chagrined,
standing outside the locked bathroom door,
wearing only a pair of dark blue rayon socks.
And it's a small leap of the mind to imagine
that blue-socked naked bum wondering
if what's coming up behind him isn't what
he desires most, after all: such are the signs
defeat puts on your body, in your mind.
And if he should conquer the wife that night,
it will be a strange threesome in their bed:
this sore-assed loser, his bottom in the air;
the sneer of defeat, riding his butt hard;
and the little screaming woman they drive crazy.

Outside the Paul Laurence Dunbar House, the Grifter Sees Us Coming

His story is amazing, told in a rush:
something about his car breaking down,
losing his job because of it, and of course,
the inevitable wife and kids waiting in it
(car? job? life?) for his return. But
here is the wild part: when we hesitate,
he pours forth a sluice of numbers, banking
on self-abasement to hold our interest—
the phone where he works (ah, *used* to work;
c.f., the car), home phone, social security
number, his *wife's* social security number,
bra size—we stop him at the kids' social
security numbers, and he breaks down, cries,
this big strong lug in an Indiana University
sweatshirt, tears backed up in his eyes
for years, a lump in his voice from the college
of hard knocks, as he gestures in frustration:
the car, the boss, the lifelong procession
of the inexplicable—you know, brother
(turning to you), you know, surely, though
he can't, that white boy next to you, who
turns now to watch how you play it: play
it well, my brother, play it right into my
hands, even as I let my eye grow cold,
measuring you: you are mine now, sucker,

you hesitated while I drove the wedge
between. Now I'm giving you a schedule
of repayment, amortized, even as I take
the folded cash: the white boy's set of bills
is thinner, as his blood is thinner: he saw
it quicker, that he'd lost, and cut his
losses like the white folk do, brother,
knowing not our game. But you, you stood,
billfold out, in the middle of my gaze:
sucker, you are mine, all mine.

"Schindler's List"

A man makes a film.
He is a Jew, a midwestern
Jew, from Cincinnati.
He knows as much as I do
about the Holocaust,

learned the same way:
newsreels, mostly, film—
the power of the image
on celluloid eclipsing
the power of the word.

Already, we are brothers,
brothers in the facile.
Yet he did not forget, or
not hear the word spoken
in his grandmother's kitchen,

the parlor where grandpa
rocked and smoked. He
remembered, and when time
came for him to turn his
face to God for forgiveness—

if only for his films—
like so many of us he

faltered first, then turned.
He did not stand free,
speaking only to the sky,

his tears falling back
to earth—anyway, hadn't
DeMille done all that?—
but wherever he stood or sat,
or bent and moaned,

wherever he prayed to be
allowed to speak, to show
the beautiful dead eyes
that he, too, remembers,
that he, too, loves:

wherever this goes on
in him, it goes on in me,
too. Always, we are
brothers in the facile
humiliations, not

history's. Afterwards,
he may take a girl
to parties on a yacht—
who knows what a man
so rich can do? And I

will go my way, not
rich, in love with failure.

Yet he is humiliated,
too, no one is spared
in this century, and I

should love myself,
what gods I know tell
me: I know it's true.
But the world that made
him, made me, too.

III

Foolish Countenances

The Body Is the Flower

So bondage is a big part of it, after all—
that old art of rendering a lover submissive:
a tactic, a strategy. Denying somebody's body
the power to move denies that body the power
to be believed. Isn't that what's so sexual?
The intimate plea? The fear you can't go back?

Until your lover throws you over on your back.
Maybe a woman becomes a man, then. After all,
it's the head games that conjure up the sexual:
which one agrees, this time, to be submissive;
which one straps on the fetishes, the powers,
we make to make the body yield up the body . . .

O the rendering, the surrendering of the body!
We so much want to go back, all the way back . . .
You stand before a mirror, naked, the power
of someone's eyes, words, erasing you, the all
you claim to be. Belief can be so submissive:
desire, not truth. But being believed is sexual

vantage: the crying out, the echo, the sexual
need you never knew could subjugate the body . . .
So you cry out at the idea of her, submissive,
yes, her hands your hands, *yes,* leading you back,
her voice your voice, *o god,* eyes lips cunt all
mirroring, *yes,* the glory, *o god yes,* the power . . .

Later, you wipe off the remnants of the power
with Kleenex. When you get down to the sexual
level, you get sexually levelled, that's all:
doesn't discipline make a believer of the body?
You whisper no name but hers in the going back.
Tomorrow, it will be her turn to be submissive:

the ties that bind render you both submissive.
You'll need her to believe your plea, her power;
she'll need you to escort her all the way back,
before the life alongside this life, her body
alongside yours: ravenous, indifferent, sexual.
There, anything might happen, anything at all,

if all you need is to be believed. The power
of the sexual plea masquerades as the submissive
act. The body is the flower of the going back.

Ghosts

My mother lifts the broomstick, slides the door,
then steps out onto the small concrete slab.
The night is cool. The leaves begin to roar.

"So nice to be outside. It's such a bore—
TV, trying to wait up for your Dad."
She puts the broomstick back, closes the door,

and turns, smoothing the sweater that she wore
the day her mother died. "I'm such a crab!"
We laugh, embrace. The leaves begin to roar.

Sometimes, the ghosts we seek to banish soar
above the castle walls . . . Our spirits flag.
We lift our broomsticks, open all the doors:

"I love you," she whispers, "I loved you more."
The night is cool. My heart's a lonely hag.
I hold her close. The leaves begin to roar.

This darkness is a black shelf, where we store
the half-lit photographs that make us mad.
I fly home through the bitter night; leaves roar.
She props the broomstick so it bars the door.

Halloween, 1992

An Ars Poetica for You

This is what I love, the charged moment,
the moment of revelation, intimacy,
the words in italics. To let someone know
what it is one wants, or needs, or is:
this is what I long to describe to you,
though scared, suddenly alone in the world,
the cold wind of the spaces between us
blowing through me as a raw afternoon
blows through wet laundry. This is what I am,
then, a line of old socks, pajamas,
underwear dancing in the grayness like
Matisse's cut-outs of the last years,
a spot of color here, a likely form there;
yet it is the old man's gaiety I feel,
watching as the world recedes from him.
There is pleasure in this, and wisdom;
still, it is the movement of declining life,
no longer presenting to his beloved
his fear. And so I turn back to you,
declining that pleasure, that wisdom,
though the effort to reach you is so enormous
I arrive gasping, my head on your thigh
the head of a drowning man, a shipwrecked man,
who could be saved by you but who appears
to you only in the grayest of light.
He counterfeits himself to look true,

who knows that at the beginning of love
one imitates the beginning, the infant need;
or that a spot of color, a likely shape is all;
or that his voice may not sound pleasing
as he whispers his urgency to you: *Do*
that. Do it that way. Oh god, that way.

To My Daughter, Sleeping

The world is beautiful, I say to you,
as we look out on morning rain, or pet
the baby goat. The world is beautiful.
Half drunk with a desire for sleep, I point
your finger at the moon, and whisper, *Moon.*
You laugh, I laugh. The world *is* beautiful . . .
Your mother says you got the night from me.
It's true: you come alive under the moon.
Hunting down the darkened streets for joy
that matches yours, you find it each second:
you know the world is beautiful. I know
only a drive, the three of us adrift
in time, you dreaming beside the bare breast,
will calm you down, allow us all to rest.
But then you're up early, crying, *Sun!*
I claim you, too! (as Mom-*ma* claims the sun).
A blue and pink world, green and gold, and white—
dazzlingly white, then shadowless, a noon
you blink at, face: the world is beautiful
in daylight, too, no blurred edges, no fuss
about what is or isn't. The sun glares,
waters your eyes, but you must understand
the sun, also. The world is beautiful.

Guides

It was on Southampton Row, after a late dinner.
Near an electric fire in the restaurant window,
I pulled my gloves on, as Ringo Starr walked by.
Leather jacket, handcuff hanging on a sleeve,
wife in a gold Mickey Mouse leopard-skin coat.
And lit a fag, same as any bloke who'd got lucky . . .
The son of a bitch.
                              "Do you see it?"
I'm myself again, the mean voice at my elbow comes
from an old woman wrapping her head in a scarf:
a guide's voice. In London, you pay per grain,
per pea. "Sure," I nod, wondering what I owe;
and smile, and push the door. But she calls out,
as I go, as how she'll more than likely hum
"Lady Madonna" the way home. I look in her eyes
this time, and nod, and go, and do the same.

Turista

So I travel to Firenze, and what do I see?
The past, or my version of it. The Guelphs
and the Ghibellines; the Bears and the Packers—
it's all the same to me: men fated to find
meaning in their violence. I steal down
the Via Proconsolo, try to imagine standing
in darkness atop the stone of one's house,
watching the fires below me, watching men,
singly or in packs, running and shouting—
and once in a while, under the streetlight,
as it were, of another's torch, witnessing
a *stiletto* flash, curses adding themselves
to the pleading and cries of the damned . . .
How the heart pores over this city's story:
old Jacopo de' Pazzi's demise comes to mind,
who coveted untold wealth, Medici wealth—
they tortured, hanged him, blamed his corpse
for bad weather, dug it up and flogged it,
dragged it through the city, then propped it
against his own doors, using its decomposing
head for a knocker, while yelling obscenities,
and the fifteenth-century Florentine version
of "Honey, I'm home!" Of course, Angelico,
the Duomo, Brunelleschi, too: in the *pietra
forte* of Santo Spirito, the raucous shouts
grow faint, and ascending San Marco's steps

for the first time, to the earthly paradise
of *The Annunciation,* I stood next to a dozen
other tourists, neither foolish nor fearful
among the whispering, just completely alone.
There were other days, less passionate, less
full of myself. Days spent whacking mosquitoes,
or searching for a *Herald-Tribune,* or a *Times.*
Bought a chess set along the Ponte Vecchio,
for the comedy of its pieces—Donatello's
David, Botticelli's "Venus," the whole gang . . .
It's oxidizing in my closet. Guzzled *Chianti,*
cappuccino. In short, I began to live there.

Portals

1

Hawthorne listed to the right
when he walked, or might have.
His head was cocked, listening
to the infernal sounds seeping,
gas from the past's dark sewer.

It's not hard to see how a soul
can begin to devour itself,
how it makes confession a line
it will not cross. A denying soul
will tell you almost anything:

what one has whispered to me
includes its proud insistence
on the story within the story,
the lie within the lie. So,
you take a sequence of events,

keep the real story in your mind,
as you describe a false story,
often along the lines of emotion
that accompanied the real story—
perhaps a truth more true.

Eventually, this marks your mind.
Sure, there's the power of it, working
quite literally like an aphrodisiac,

thus ensuring its continued use.
Oh, and you want to show the past

a thing or two, even if you hate
the past. The problem is, we forget
life. We remember dates, places,
but we forget the languages
that were our fiercest allies,

as we approached each individual
abyss. The language of the hunt,
for example, must have been
a powerful language. How women
survived its awful power

is a language that is silent,
we are told. An unhappy fate,
yet it teaches us the language,
powerful, of keeping others safe
from the powers of language.

We sit in middle age, the snapped-
off languages lying close,
like toys we have succeeded
in demolishing. Will touch
proceed from this, or scorn—

scorn of the human? And that's
the story within the story:
the scorn or love that once
were different, yet now
mean one and the same thing.

2

But we move now to our own time,
where the fear of coming
in her mouth is a fear
of power: who gains the power
to release the power?

Will we rely on them,
or they on us? We want
to rely, because there's no come
like that one, no moan louder
than the one inside.

But will we be sacrificed
after the usual year?
What list of attributes must we
embody to appease, and please,
them? Women are bad

teachers: they know more but
this makes them willing to accept
our not knowing. We strut,
we get a false sense of
ourselves, our worth, we get

the ax. And no one likes it,
protests to the contrary:
we make ourselves the more
unlikable before we'll give in
so meekly to our fate,

thus ensuring it. We live,
always seeking a way out.
And, let's face it, in.
It *is* a force, a jet.
It *is* a recombining, wet.

3

In the boat of the city,
we look through portals
at nature: the November sky,
the obligatory bare tree—
framed for us for an instant,

then vanishing, not from view,
but mind. Our cruise ship,
City of Cincinnati, floats
through the brown wreckage
of its century. Once I drove

the city on a fine fall night,
mapmaking, trying to get a feel
for distance, direction—for
destiny, I guess. The river runs
west, actually, into the sun,

then drops south to Louisville.
Sunset can turn the river
into cobalt blue, ultramarine—
even, one night, a purple-orange,
produced by chemicals in the air,

no doubt. It isn't the sea.
It doesn't have the great expanse
to match the great extension
of the human spirit, those spirits
who live by the sea say

of the sea, and of themselves.
Still, someone may be a part
of a small place, and yet part
of a larger—even as a river
still runs south to the sea.

4

Prayer is a form of concentration
meant to lead you upward
from wherever you are. I
have been leading all my life
sideways, to something I've always

known was there. Not "above,"
or "below": in fact, I got vertigo,
trying to balance all that. I
fell back, against a tree—
then, holding my head, turned,

half stumbling against the side
of the world, the part of God
that waits for someone as smart
as me, someone that smart.
Prayer is a form of detection,

and detection a form of prayer:
my hand poked through the world,
and I straightened up by myself.
Detectives reassure us because
the city flows within and without

them, the City of God. Bullitt,
in San Francisco, never heard
the roar of the ocean behind him—
he thought the sound was inside him.
He was a good cop. Popeye Doyle,

on the other hand, believed
the city existed only as a set
against which his bigger-than-life
impersonations played out. Proving
that egomania isn't the way

to the clearing in which you kneel,
studying something in the light,
the sound of the world the same
as the sound at the back
of your thoughts. Stopping there,

all you have to do is look up,
to see what you knew was waiting
for you to notice. And you notice,
partly in an old way you'd forgotten,
but mostly in a new way.

Singing in the Rain

The earth was a smear before my blank stare,
or my blank stare was a smear. Either way,
it was raining bootheels, a dance I danced
away from, or liked to think I did. Nature
appealed to me in the abstract, but in the everyday
I was disconnected from the great daisy chain
of Being, covered my ass. It rained all winter,

and it would be years before I lifted my eyes
from poems. Not that I thought they could save me,
nothing could save me, I knew that, and yet
we dream . . . You spoke of "Lucky Pierre," entered
and entering, sandwiched between what gives
and What gives? That was an important lesson
in loneliness, and I swallowed it. Like Frank O'Hara,

I wanted a friend who could show up on a bad day
with a smile and a blow job for me (but female:
those of us who love women have yet to learn
to lie in the cold gray light of each other)—
and then it happened, and there was much guilt
all around. It was later I began to lift my head
from the book of the world, the revelation of a woman,

to notice that the world was not opaque, in fact,
that it was disappearing, even as mist before my eyes,

its fierce dancing belaboring another head, its cold
stream of consciousness not my own, then again,
my own. I was within and without me, and the world
was without me in a big way, and within me in a way
no being can make another being say Yes like that.

Green Fuse

Our children always defeat us.
It's simply a rule of life.
And how much we want this to happen
is seen in the grief of those
whose children die before them.

At some point I gave in.
The return was this great energy.
For the first time I can feel
something of what drove Whitman
down those streets, what it means

to be a member of this fallible
human community, to stand
up into the wild air above us,
and not deny this, to feel
the sexual power of all

that is not us, and not deny.
To feel the generative force
of every being on the planet
is beyond me, at this point,
but I won't deny what I like

ever again. I turn to the face
of a child, but it is my child,

her face a mirror of my own.
You are too much for me, I say,
holding her close, so glad of this.

Romantic Love

Love doesn't go away.
You can't tell love no,
then expect it to vanish,
as if you never have a thought
again of limbs in motion,
bodies at rest. Love,

once there, is always love,
always there. Turn away
the lover's great emotion,
his body chafes, as *No*
chafes a child. Then a thought
of her, and worlds vanish,

as a child's hurt will vanish,
soothed by a *Yes* of love.
Yeats said he had a thought
of loving in the old high way,
but Maud Gonne said no,
with a quick hand motion,

a quick impatient motion,
that caused his heart to vanish.
But love didn't vanish, no,
it became a paradigm of love:
he made a map of the way
we become ourselves. The thought,

the sheer amount of thought,
he diverted from his emotion
staggers the mind. The Way
is a way to vanish
from the grasp of Love,
a way of saying no

that is the opposite of no.
The unsettling thought
there might be a higher love
engenders an emotion
we want to vanish.
The way is only the way;

we know thought is emotion.
We long to vanish in love;
that way is our way.

To His Book

Go, little mirror. You hold up to me
only desire, not what I long to see.

Notes

"The Man Who Broke Jackson Pollock's Nose": The incident described in this poem is imaginary.

"Quotes": Except for Lincoln's famous remark about "Fighting Joe" Hooker, made in response to dispatches sent from what Hooker called his "Headquarters in the saddle," the quotes and speakers here are invented.

"Portrait of Man with Blue Mug": "Bresson's priest" refers to Robert Bresson's film *Diary of a Country Priest*.

"Foolish Countenances": The phrase "Foolish Countenances," used as the title for part 3, refers to a remark attributed to Lao Tzu by the historian Ssu-ma Ch'ien: "I have heard it said that a good merchant hides his store in a safe place and appears to be devoid of possessions, while a gentleman, though endowed with great virtue, wears a foolish countenance."

"Portals": "Bullitt" and "Popeye Doyle" refer to characters in the movies *Bullitt* and *The French Connection*.

The James Dickey Contemporary Poetry Series
Edited by Richard Howard

Error and Angels
Maureen Bloomfield

Portrait in a Spoon
James Cummins

The Land of Milk and Honey
Sarah Getty

All Clear
Robert Hahn

Traveling in Notions:
The Stories of Gordon Penn
Michael J. Rosen

United Artists
S. X. Rosenstock